FEB 2 7 2019

GENETIC DISEASES
AND GENE THERAPIES

DEPRESSION

Richard Spilsbury

rosen publishing's
rosen
central®

New York

Published in 2019 by The Rosen Publishing Group, Inc.
29 East 21st Street
New York, NY 10010

First Edition

Produced for Rosen by Calcium Creative Ltd.
Editors for Calcium: Sarah Eason and Kris Hirschmann
Designer: Simon Borrough
Picture researcher: Rachel Blount

Photo credits: Cover: Orange Deer: bottom right; Andrii Muzyka: bottom; Suzanne Tucker: main; Inside: Shutterstock: Africa Studio: p. 17; Andrey Popov: pp. 12, 15; Artellia: p. 26; Daxiao Productions: p. 34; Bumble Dee: p. 42; GeK: p. 38; Image Point Fr: p. 31; Iordani: p. 19b; Izf: p. 43; JN-chantalao: p. 30; KieferPix: p. 28; Maradon 333: p. 41; Newphotoservice: p. 6; Novak.elcic: p. 33; Pathdoc: p. 21; Patrice6000: p. 10; Pixelheadphoto digitalskillet: p. 44; Kirill Polikarpov: p. 16; Pressmaster: p. 27; Sasa Prudkov: p. 8; Rost9: p. 11; Science Photo: p. 36; Kenneth Sponsler: p. 23; Anatolii Stoiko: p. 19t; Tommaso79: p. 4; Vectorfusionart: p. 35; Vgstockstudio: p. 25; Ysuel: p. 7; Wikimedia Commons: Rama: p. 39; Ed Uthman from Houston, TX, USA: p. 20.

Cataloging-in-Publication Data

Names: Spilsbury, Richard.
Title: Depression / Richard Spilsbury.
Description: New York : Rosen Central, 2019. | Series: Genetic diseases and gene therapies | Includes glossary and index.
Identifiers: LCCN ISBN 9781508182771 (pbk.) | ISBN 9781508182764 (library bound)
Subjects: LCSH: Depression, Mental—Juvenile literature. | Depression in children—Juvenile literature.
Classification: LCC RC537.S646 2019 | DDC 616.85'27—dc23

Manufactured in the United States of America

Contents

Chapter 1

What Is Depression?

Normal life is full of high and low moods. Feeling low or sad is natural and can be caused by many things. For example, you might feel sad because of something not going your way, running out of money, worrying about exam results, the cancellation of a much-anticipated event, or receiving bad news, such as a family member becoming sick. Many people will say they are feeling "depressed" about things during periods when they are feeling down. However, this is different from when someone has a medical condition called depression.

A person suffering from depression may look fine on the outside, but the outer looks do not always match the inner reality. Some people are very good at masking their depression.

Extreme Low

It seems as though you are under a dark cloud when you are feeling low. You may struggle to cope with normal events, be on the verge of tears all the time, and feel cut off from others. People with depression experience lows that are often much lower than this, with feelings of intense sadness and bleakness. They may experience these feelings over long periods, when their low mood completely dominates their lives and even makes them feel scarily out of control. Depression dampens a person's ability to take pleasure in anything, to do everyday things, and to take any interest in activities.

Mental Illness

It is fairly easy to spot a physical illness, such as measles, and for doctors to test whether someone has a heart disease or brain tumor. However, mental illnesses or mental health disorders are caused by how our brains make us feel and react. They are often less obvious than physical illnesses, even though they can make anyone feel just as bad as a physical illness would. Depression is a mental illness, which sometimes makes it tricky to spot and diagnose. However, anyone can develop depression and it can be passed from parents to children, through their genes. Like many physical illnesses, depression can be treated and does not last forever.

GENE STORIES

"When my depression spirals out of control, I want to stay in my room and hide from the world. I feel like I am on a slippery, downward slope. It is like I am at my most emotional, to the point that others might consider me crazy, but also feeling empty inside and emotionless. I am at war, fighting a battle against myself."
—Jodie, age twenty-one

Psychological Symptoms

When someone has a broken leg or heart problem, people rarely say things to them like "Snap out of it" or "Pull yourself together." However, they might do this to someone who suffers from depression. Because it is an illness of the mind, some people think that depression is somehow not a genuine health condition, is a sign of weakness, or is trivial in comparison to physical health problems. However, depression is an illness with a range of typical symptoms—the signs of an illness or condition—like any other.

Some of the symptoms of depression are psychological, which means they are related to the emotional and mental state of a person. A person with depression may feel:

- a continuous low mood or sadness

- hopeless and helpless: the future seems bleak and they feel they can do little to make it better

- low self-esteem: this means low self-respect, self-confidence, and morale, and little pride or belief in one's abilities

- trouble sleeping, or insomnia

- tearful

Increased anxiety and psychotic symptoms can have a severe impact on people with depression.

- guilt-ridden: that they have done something wrong or bad to others, causing themselves to feel this way

- irritable and intolerant of others

- no motivation or interest in things and no enjoyment out of life

- difficulty in making decisions

- increased anxiety: they are worried, tense, restless, agitated, and frightened

Psychotic thoughts may be a trick of the mind, but can seem intensely real.

Psychotic Symptoms

When we have dreams, some can seem incredibly real and vivid, even though that dream situation is rather unrealistic. Some people with depression often hear, see, or believe things that aren't real, even when they are awake. For example, they might become convinced that they have done something really bad, such as injured someone or stolen something, or that someone is watching them or poisoning their food. Irrational thoughts and feelings of being under threat are called paranoia. Sometimes people have hallucinations, too, such as imagining that they hear voices or seeing things that are not really happening. Paranoia and hallucinations are types of psychotic symptoms.

Bipolar Disorder

Some people have alternating episodes of depression and mania during their lives. Mania, or manic episodes, are lengthy periods when someone feels incredibly high and bursting with energy. A person in that state is typically happy, distracted, very active, very awake, taking risks, talkative in a garbled way, and distracted. When people experience both depression and mania, they have bipolar disorder, which used to be known as manic depression. People with depression do not have manic episodes. Depression and bipolar disorder are the two major mood disorders.

Physical and Social Symptoms

Although depression is primarily a mental condition, people with this illness can have a range of physical symptoms, too. These can have a big impact on a person's health, well-being, and social life.

Physical Symptoms

Physical symptoms of depression can include constipation—when people cannot pass solid waste easily. As well, women can sometimes experience changes to their menstrual cycle, such as irregular or

People with depression often avoid social activities. They may remove themselves from people and situations they once enjoyed.

heavier periods. People with depression often move or speak more slowly than usual. They lack the energy to do even the simplest tasks, such as getting out of bed or showering. This is partly because depression can lead to disturbed sleep patterns. People with depression may find it difficult to fall asleep and may have insomnia. They may also lose their appetite and lose weight, or they may eat more than usual and gain weight.

Sadly, some people have such extreme, intense depression that the only solution they believe they have is to self-harm. This is when people injure themselves, for example by cutting their skin. Other people may become suicidal and attempt to kill themselves as a result of their depression.

Social Symptoms

Have you ever skipped an event because you were feeling sad, troubled, or tired? Depression can effectively shut people down in any social setting due to a lack of self-esteem, confidence, and energy. People who have depression may also struggle with work or school. They may not be able to complete tasks, plan, or make changes to improve their productivity. They may have poor attendance and skip commitments with little warning. People with depression may avoid social interaction, even with their best friends and at their favorite sports or clubs. They may neglect their interests and hobbies. Life at home can become very strained because people with depression have difficulty participating in family life and relating normally to family members.

GENE STORIES

"Depression makes me lonely. Happy people aren't lonely, are they? Time slows down and negative thoughts get louder, so my sadness gets sadder still, and I feel lonelier. I might think things like, 'I don't like myself, so no one else should like me either.' That leads to more negative thoughts, like 'What is wrong with me? I am bad. People should stay away, otherwise my badness will infect them, too.' "
—Paul, age twenty-nine

Chapter 2

Why Do People Develop Depression?

At least 10 percent of all people in the United States will experience depression at some point in their lives. It can strike anyone, at any age, including children. Remarkably, for such a common illness, scientists and doctors are not certain of exactly what causes depression. However, they do know that the brain is the root cause of the intense lows in people with depression.

The Brain

Nearly everything we do is controlled by our brain—the headquarters of the nervous system. This network of nerves carries information to and from the rest of your body. It controls, among other things, the senses and movement. Each brain contains about 100 billion nerve cells called neurons, which are organized into different regions with different jobs to do. For example, the cerebrum responds to the world around us and controls speech and vision. The limbic system, which contains the amygdala, hippocampus, and hypothalamus, is responsible for all the emotions we feel and things we remember. The limbic system motivates us to do things and to experience fear, update and add new memories, control emotional reactions, and moderate sleep patterns and hunger, among many other functions.

Your brain controls your senses, moods, and perceptions of yourself and others.

Message Flow

Bundles of neurons carry many messages to and from different parts of the body. Neurons are special cells with a long part called an axon on one side and tufty parts called dendrites on the other. Nerve messages move as tiny, very fast bursts of electricity through the axon of one neuron. At the end of the axon, they reach a very small gap called a synapse that they must cross to reach the dendrites of the next neuron. The messages cross the gap using special chemicals called neurotransmitters. Scientists think that depression involves lower-than-normal amounts of neurotransmitters such as serotonin in the limbic system. An imbalance of serotonin affects a person's sleepiness and his or her ability to learn and remember, and may cause mood distortion.

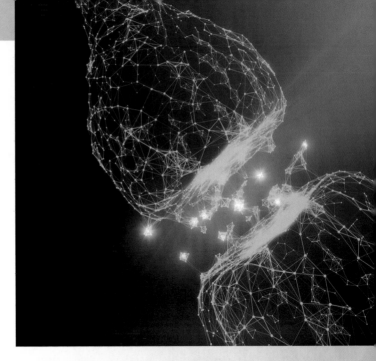

Neurotransmitters are chemicals produced in neurons that flood the brain to keep messages moving to and from brain parts.

Inconclusive Proof

The evidence for serotonin being the cause is not definite. When doctors prescribe serotonin to people with depression, it does not always improve mood. If it does, it takes at least a month to work. Also, studies searching for low serotonin levels in the brains of depressed people have been inconclusive. The brain is a very complicated organ in which neurons and neurotransmitters interact in many ways, and can work very differently between individuals. Despite these lingering questions, however, it remains likely that serotonin blocks chains of negative thoughts, alters the way the limbic system processes emotions, and helps people see the positive in situations.

Stresses and Changes

The risk of developing depression is strongly affected by the emotional surroundings and stressful events that someone is exposed to. These things can massively lower self-esteem and the ability to cope with life's ups and downs. For this reason, depression can develop more easily in people who are often in an emotionally negative and/or high-stress environment.

Childhood Experiences

When bad things happen to a young person, they can have a major impact on their self-esteem and ability to cope with certain situations and emotions. For example, if children are repeatedly punished for things such as wetting the bed or getting things wrong, they may grow up to think that they are worthless and can't do anything right.

Depression is about twice as common in the homeless population as it is among those with more stable living situations.

During childhood, physical, emotional, and sexual abuse, along with neglect, are often linked to major depression later on, too. Other root causes of depression in childhood include having an unstable family, such as when parents are going through a long, troubled divorce. Going through lots of smaller challenging experiences can sometimes have a greater impact than going through one major experience. Such repeating patterns are stored as powerful negative memories and emotions by the limbic system.

Difficult Events

Although children are most susceptible to the effects of stressful, unwelcome, and traumatic events, these situations can trigger depression in people at any age. If someone you know has ever lost a job, you probably saw the emotional and physical toll that event had on them. For example, it may have raised such worrying questions as "How will I feed my family?" or "Will I lose my home?" Other difficult events that have a powerful emotional impact include the intense sadness when a loved one dies, when a relationship ends, or when someone is bullied or physically assaulted. Some people develop depression after big changes. These may even be changes that seem like they should make people happy, such as moving to a new country or getting married. Every individual is affected in different ways by events and changes. The way we react to them depends on how we deal with such events, and how much emotional support we seek or receive from others after the event.

GENE STORIES

"My depression probably started when I was a child. My mother had mental health problems because she struggled to cope, and my father brushed her feelings under the carpet. I couldn't understand why she would be in tears on a daily basis, and probably subconsciously started to think it was my fault."
—Darryl, age forty-four

Health and Depression

Being sick can make anyone feel lower than usual. This is normal. However, some types of illnesses can increase the risk of developing the more serious condition of depression. Health problems that last longer than three months, such as rheumatoid arthritis, or life-threatening illnesses, such as cancer, can be difficult to manage. The deep uncertainty and stress about one's health, the impact on family and lifestyle, and many other things, may greatly lower a person's mood. Other illnesses directly cause depression through their physical effects on a person's body, rather than through related worry and stress.

Brain Disorders

Dementia is a loss of memory and changes to thinking, problem-solving, and language abilities associated with brain damage caused, for example, by Alzheimer's disease. Parkinson's disease is a condition characterized by slow movement, tremors (shaking), and body stiffness caused by weakening neurons in the center of the brain. Some doctors believe that depression may be a symptom of the early stages of both brain disorders, whereas others see depression as their cause.

Thyroid Conditions

The thyroid is a gland near the front of your neck that produces hormones and proteins regulating many body systems. Hormones from the thyroid regulate how fast body cells work, which can have an impact on everything from heart rate and body temperature to intestinal and brain activity. Researchers have found that people with underactive thyroids that do not make make enough hormones are more likely to have low moods, gain weight, be tired, and have poor concentration—all symptoms of depression.

Mental Health

Some people develop depression as a result of experiencing mental health disorders such as anxiety, eating disorders such as bulimia or anorexia, or post-traumatic stress disorder (PTSD).

A combination of mobility loss, anxiety about the future, and poor self-esteem can cause depression in some individuals.

Gene Genies

In a 2014 study at Mount Sinai Medical Center in New York City, researchers investigated the impact that stress has on depression. They stressed non-aggressive mice by introducing aggressive mice into their cage. In blood tests, they found that the stressed mice produced large amounts of a chemical called interleukin-6 (IL-6). This chemical is normally produced by white blood cells in the immune system—the body's defensive shield—during attack by invaders such as allergens. In this case, the increased IL-6 resulted from stress hormones. The raised IL-6 increased fatigue, changed the appetite, reduced social interaction, and produced other depression-associated symptoms in the mice. Researchers then tested blood from volunteers with depression and also found raised amounts of IL-6 in some. This evidence supports the idea that depression can be an allergic reaction to stress.

Other Causes of Depression

There are many other things that trigger or kick-start depression in different people. Scientists have identified some of the most common factors.

Drugs

People on heavy medication to treat all kinds of health problems can sometimes develop depression as a side effect. For example, some people with severe acne take a drug called isotretinoin that reduces the amount of oil produced by skin, as this oiliness can lead to pimples. However, depression is one of its side effects, so its use has to be carefully monitored by doctors.

Recreational legal drugs such as alcohol and tobacco, along with illegal drugs such as marijuana and cocaine, can also lead to depression. Although people might initially use them to make themselves feel better or to distract themselves, these drugs generally make them feel worse overall. Many have psychotic effects, as well as serious physical health effects such as heart damage. Users may also have low self-esteem associated with drug use.

Drugs to cure the symptoms of one condition can cause chemical changes that trigger depression.

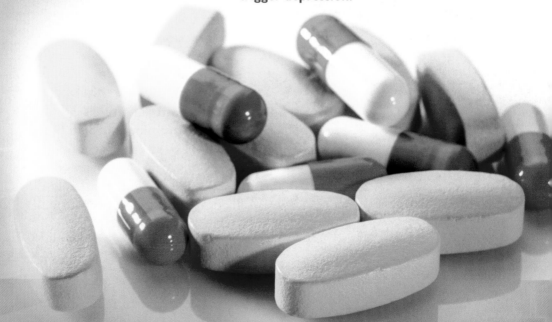

Postpartum Depression

As many as one in ten women experience depression after having a baby, and some men have this postpartum depression, also. Most new parents are tired and anxious after bringing a new person into the world, and some have the "baby blues" for days to weeks. The

Becoming a new parent is overwhelming to most people. But for some, the joy is almost completely masked by depressive symptoms.

symptoms include sadness, low mood, exhaustion, insomnia, and difficulty bonding with their baby. These symptoms normally go away as people get used to their new family lives. However, in people with postpartum depression, the symptoms start gradually and last longer or start later. Some may have much more intense symptoms, such as psychotic thoughts about hurting their baby.

Seasonal Affective Disorder

Most of us feel happy and more energetic in sunnier, lighter seasons, and sleep longer and eat more in colder, darker seasons. In a type of depression called seasonal affective disorder (SAD), people experience a much greater effect on their mood and energy levels than normal, usually in fall and winter. However, some get SAD as summer arrives. Scientists have found that the brains of people with SAD often have altered levels of serotonin, and produce higher-than-usual levels of the hormone melatonin, which makes us sleep.

Chapter 3

Inheriting Depression

When studying adopted people with depression, scientists found their chance of developing depression was higher if their biological parent had depression, too. This and other findings suggest that a major reason for people developing depression is inheriting it from others in their family through their genes.

What Are Genes?

Genes are the blueprint of instructions found inside every cell that tell it how to develop, grow, and function. Cells are the building blocks of any living thing. The instructions are not written down, but instead are elaborate structures made up of a substance called DNA. It looks somewhat like a ladder twisted into a spiral. Each rung of the ladder is made from a particular sequence of chemicals, like a string of letters completing a word. These "words" instruct the body's cells, just like words in an instruction book provide written directions. Each person's genes contain all the instructions for living that they will ever need. But only the genes that are actually turned on and active have any effect. Every person contains the gene instructions involved in depression. However, because these genes are usually turned off, only a small percentage of people will go on to develop the condition.

Set of Chromosomes

Thousands of genes are twisted and packed tightly into chromosomes inside cells. Each cell in our bodies contains 23 pairs of chromosomes, making 46 altogether. When living things reproduce sexually, one chromosome of each pair from a male joins with another pair from a female to produce new pairs in their offspring. Each person inherits a unique set of chromosomes with its own combination of genes from his or her mother and father. Particular mixes of genes can make it more likely for a person to develop a particular illness, such as depression.

Chemical codes in the genes provide the blueprint for each person.

GENE STORIES

"I was sick of people saying my teenage daughter was just moody. I had seen her lying in bed for months, not eating, and heard her say she was a failure and could not go on. I recognized it as severe depression because that's what I'd had years earlier. And I remember my own mother standing in the kitchen, crying helplessly. Depression was no doubt triggered by various stresses in our lives, like me going away to college, but it was already part of our biology."

—*Anna, age fifty-six*

Depression can run in families partly as a result of genes that increase the risk of someone getting the illness.

19

Genes and Medical Conditions

Many genes have different forms or variants that are slightly different in the DNA coding. These differences determine a person's physical traits. For example, if you inherited a gene variant from your parents that produces brown eyes, then the cells in your developing eye produced a brown-colored part. These differences occur because of changes or mutations in the DNA code. They can lead not just to simple traits like eye color, but to many medical conditions as well.

How Mutations Happen

Mutations can happen when DNA is not copied properly as cells divide during growth and reproduction. They can also happen when people are exposed to harmful chemicals. For example, chemicals in smoke can damage DNA and cause mutations in lung cells, leading to cancer. Some mutations are beneficial, some are neutral and have no effect, and others can cause a disease.

Genetic Diseases

Some genetic diseases, such as cystic fibrosis, can only happen if a child inherits the same mutation from each parent. Others, such as Huntington's disease, are inherited if a child receives only one mutated Huntington's gene from a parent. Other genetic diseases, such as Down syndrome, result from chromosome changes during

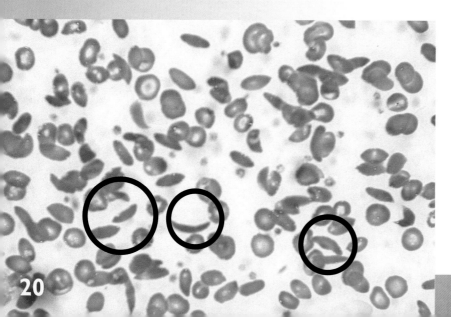

A disease called sickle cell anemia is caused by mutated red blood cells that are sharp instead of round.

Although catching a cold or the flu is not a genetic condition, some people are more prone to these illnesses than others due to their genetics.

Gene Genies

In 2017, Dutch and Russian scientists identified a gene called NKPD1, mutations of which may play an important role in depression. They studied a set of more than three thousand closely related people called the Erasmus Rucphen Family (ERF) living in an isolated part of the Netherlands. The ERF is made up of the descendants of just twenty-two families from the eighteenth century, with a very restricted set of genes. This is due to most marriages occuring only within the ERF. Responses to questionnaires about health symptoms suggested that there is a very high incidence of depression in the group. The NKPD1 mutation was found more often in DNA samples from people in the ERF with symptoms of depression than those without. Scientists think that NKPD1 helps control production of a fatty substance that is important in mental health.

reproduction. Depression does not fall into any of these neat categories. In other words, there is no single depression gene mutation causing the disease. Scientists think depression is polygenic, or involving many genes, which interact in different ways in different individuals. No one is genetically predetermined to develop depression, but the particular blend of genes passed down from their parents can put them at greater risk of developing the illness.

Running in the Family

The chances of someone developing depression depend in part on that person's genetic makeup. The discovery of the genetic connection was due to research that determined depression often runs in families.

Patterns

Scientists and doctors called epidemiologists study populations of people and examine medical records to find patterns of illness. They focus on those patterns in families to estimate their heritability, or the likelihood that their cause is due to genes. For example, in one specific family, one family member has an illness. There is a higher heritability of that illness in that family than there is in the general population. Therefore, it is likely that genes play a significant role in spreading that illness. Epidemiologists have found that if someone has a parent or sibling who has major depression, they probably have a 20 to 30 percent chance of developing depression themselves. This is two to three times higher than an average person's risk. The risk is greater if a parent or sibling's depression occurs many times in his or her life, especially if it started in early life. The chance of developing depression is also high in people with relatives with bipolar disorder.

Gene Genies

In 2016, researchers at the University of California analyzed brain scans showing the shape and form of the limbic system in adults and their children. The limbic system is the part of the brain that processes emotions. They discovered that the heritability of the limbic system was greater from mothers to daughters than from mothers to sons, or from fathers to either gender of offspring. This finding helps to explain previous studies showing that when a mother experiences stress while pregnant, her female offspring are more likely than her male offspring to show physical changes in the limbic system.

Twin Studies

Twin studies are important to people researching the spread of disorders and diseases because twins share some or all of their genes. Identical twins share all of their genes, whereas non-identical twins share half. It stands to reason that if one identical twin develops the same condition as his or her twin, genes probably had something to do with it. If one twin has not yet developed the condition, his or her chances of doing so are higher than if they were non-identical twins or non-twin siblings.

Scientists report that if one identical twin has depression, the other twin has around a 40 to 50 percent chance of developing the condition—a much higher-than-normal risk.

Studying the heritability of depression in twins may help scientists locate and treat the genes involved in mood.

Chapter 4

Treating Depression

Before anyone can get treatment or help for their depression, they need a diagnosis. A diagnosis is when doctors and other specialists examine a patient and identify the symptoms or signs that tell them that person has a particular injury, disease, or condition.

Talking About It

When someone goes to the doctor feeling unwell, the doctor may take his or her temperature, use special blood tests, or perform other physical examinations to help diagnose what is wrong. A patient may display physical symptoms suggesting depression, but will rarely display their psychological symptoms at a consultation. To determine whether someone suffers from depression, a psychiatrist must talk to the patient and hear about these symptoms directly from them.

During these conversations, it is very important for people to describe their mood, behavior patterns, and what life is like for them day to day. Ideally, patients will have a diary or other record of their episodes of low mood and other possible depression symptoms. They will also offer some detail about anyone in their family who has depression. These details will help the psychiatrist to make a diagnosis. It can also be helpful for psychiatrists to meet and talk with relatives of patients to get a better idea of their emotional history.

Classifying Depression

Psychiatrists use national or international guidelines to help diagnose depression. Guidelines such as ICD-10 and DSM-IV are lists of standard symptoms typical of a wide range of people with depression. They include depressed mood, loss of interest or pleasure, fatigue or reduction in energy, and feelings of worthlessness and guilt. To be diagnosed, a person does not have to have every

People often bring a parent or family member with them to meet a doctor or psychiatrist. Family members can help explain and describe some of the patient's unusual behaviors.

symptom. However, having more of the symptoms on the list can indicate more severe depression.

If a psychiatrist diagnoses depression, then it is called clinical depression. More women than men are diagnosed with clinical depression, partly because women in general are more comfortable with discussing emotional changes that suggest mental illnesses. Women are also more likely than men to seek help. Psychiatrists often separate mild, moderate, and severe (or minor and major) depressive episodes based on the symptoms. This helps them to diagnose several forms of depression:

Recurrent depressive disorder: When a patient has had at least two depressive episodes

Reactive depression: When depression was caused by stressful events

Dysthymia: When patients feel low for several years without repeated depressive episodes

Psychotic depression: When symptoms involve hallucinations and/or paranoia

Talk Therapy

When you have problems, you might find it helpful to talk. In talk therapy, a patient who has depression or another mental illness talks about his or her problems with a trained professional. Those problems are usually linked to the patient's mental and emotional health. Therapists help patients approach those problems in a different way. There are different kinds of talk therapy. One type, psychotherapy, focuses on a patient's early relationships and experiences, and what impact they have on current relationships with others. Another type, Cognitive behavioral therapy (CBT), helps people identify their unhealthy, negative ideas and behaviors, and replace them with healthy, positive ones.

How CBT Works

The idea of CBT is to help people with depression or other mental illnesses figure out what triggers episodes. It then teaches them ways to cope with stress and upsetting situations. Trained CBT therapists help people break down overwhelming feelings into separate areas such as situations, thoughts, emotions, physical feelings, and actions. CBT is based on the idea that these different areas are connected. The way people think about a particular situation affects how they feel about it, and how they respond or react when it happens. For example, if people think they'll never be able to sort a

THOUGHTS
create Feelings

FEELINGS
create Behavior

HELPS to CRACK the VICIOUS CYCLE of Negative Thinking and Feeling

Cognitive Behavioral Therapy

BEHAVIOR
creates Thoughts

With cognitive behavioral therapy, therapists can help people look at problems in a helpful rather than unhelpful way.

An expert in mental illnesses can help a patient to figure out what caused his or her problems in the first place and learn how to manage any existing problems and symptoms of depression.

problem out, they are more likely to fail and feel depressed about it. But if they instead accept that everyone faces problems, and that they might be able to solve it or get help solving it, the result is generally more positive.

Patients with mild-to-moderate depression can also do CBT on their computer at home, rather than wait for therapist sessions. For example, MoodGym is a program offering quizzes, interactive games, assessments of anxiety and depression, downloadable relaxation audio, and a workbook.

GENE STORIES

"I often say that depression is like looking out at the world from inside a goldfish bowl. One of the only ways I have found to really escape the bowl is talk therapy. This helped me no end in getting the confidence I needed to get my whole family into behavioral therapy. I know they love me so much, but this therapy has really helped our relationships. Now they can spot and manage my lowest moods better and because they understand more about my illness, they can help me to solve many of my problems."
—*Zach, age twenty-two*

Antidepressants and Other Therapies

People with a simple headache often take some aspirin or acetaminophen to get rid of the pain. In a similar way, when people have depression, medication called antidepressants can help improve some of their symptoms.

How Antidepressants Work

Most antidepressants relieve symptoms of depression by affecting how neurotransmitters in the brain behave. The neurotransmitters involved are serotonin, norepinephrine, and dopamine. Different antidepressants work in different ways. For example, reuptake inhibitors—SSRIs, SNRIs, and NDRIs—prevent neurons from reabsorbing neurotransmitters after they are released to send messages in the brain. The idea is that keeping levels of neurotransmitters higher could improve communication between neurons. It could also strengthen information pathways in the limbic system that control mood. However, some scientists question whether low neurotransmitter levels actually cause depression. They wonder whether higher levels may improve depression in other ways, such as regulating the genes that control neuron growth and function.

Selective serotonin reuptake inhibitors (SSRIs), including Prozac and Zoloft, are among the most commonly prescribed antidepressants.

Impacts

Many people with depression find that antidepressants taken daily reduce the intensity of their low moods, give them more energy, and help restore their emotional balance. The changes become noticeable after about six weeks of taking the tablets. The changes are generally greater for people with more severe depressive episodes, and much less for people with mild depression. Antidepressants cause a range of side effects in different people, including nausea, vomiting, excessive sweating, high blood pressure, and insomnia. Doctors must keep a close eye on patients taking antidepressants to regulate their dosages. They must also check whether the medication has an impact on any other health conditions patients may have.

Other Therapies

Some people with severe depression gain little positive effect from CBT or antidepressants, and their condition can put their lives at risk. In such cases, doctors may suggest electroconvulsive therapy. In that treatment, an electrical current is briefly passed through the patient's brain. The patient is put under general anesthetic, so they cannot wake during the procedure. The electricity causes uncontrolled convulsions, resulting from the excessive neuron activity in the brain. Doctors think this increased activity stimulates the release of neurotransmitters and the growth of neurons. A less-drastic treatment called transcranial magnetic stimulation uses repeated pulses of a strong magnetic field into the brain from a handheld device. Like electroconvulsive therapy, this treatment is thought to stimulate neurons.

> ## GENE STORIES
>
> "I was astounded that something so insignificant as a little white pill could help me so much. I genuinely felt like a cloud had been lifted after taking antidepressants. The medication didn't make me instantly happy, but it gave me perspective, which was the thing I wanted above all else."
>
> —Nina, age forty

Chapter 5

Living with Depression

People often feel relieved in the first weeks and months after getting a medical diagnosis of depression. They finally have an official explanation for their moods and behavior and health care professionals from doctors to psychotherapists can start new programs of treatment. However, life with the illness continues after diagnosis. To help themselves cope with the illness, people must use many strategies along with medication and therapies. One of the most important strategies is taking care of themselves to make the most of their different interventions.

Stick to the Treatment

Sometimes when people with depression feel well, they are tempted to skip psychotherapy sessions or appointments, perhaps because they are time-consuming or inconvenient. They might also decide not to take their antidepressants because they don't like depending on pills. However, if they stop, depression symptoms can return. Also, even after a few days off their medication, people might go through withdrawal that includes flu-like symptoms, headaches, insomnia, and other unpleasant effects. It takes time and constant treatment to feel better with depression. Many people with depression find it empowering to learn more about the condition. This knowledge can motivate them to stick to their treatment plan.

It is critical for people with depression to monitor themselves and reach out for help as soon as symptoms emerge.

Daylight lamps can ease the symptoms of depression in people with SAD.

Spot the Warning Signs

Many things can trigger depression, so it is important to work with your doctor or therapist to learn what might trigger your symptoms. For example, people with SAD are often triggered by low light levels. They may find it helpful in winter to spend time in places with longer days, or to use daylight-simulation lamps to reduce symptoms. In the weeks before their period, some women experience unusually intense symptoms of premenstrual syndrome (PMS), such as extreme mood swings, exhaustion, and bloating which can trigger depression. Therapies such as hormone treatment and behavioral changes such as increased exercise can lessen these symptoms. Whenever or however depressive episodes begin, people should seek assistance before the symptoms spiral out of control.

Watch for Changes

People with depression need to watch out for the impacts it has on their overall health, not just for the side effects of using antidepressants. Chemical changes in the body that are associated with depression can lead to other illnesses. For example, people with depression have a higher risk of developing heart disease. One reason for this may be that the serotonin drop associated with depression may cause certain particles in the blood to stick together more frequently and cause more blockages in blood vessels.

Better Living

Most of us feel better when we eat healthy food, drink enough water, get enough sleep, and exercise. This is not surprising because we are living things with certain biological requirements for remaining both physically and mentally healthy. People with depression can moderate their symptoms significantly through better living.

Diet

When we feel low, it is tempting to reach for the potato chips and sweet treats. This is an ongoing problem for many people with depression. They may often eat junk foods high in fat and sugar that can make their symptoms worse. For example, people may get a sugar rush of energy from carbohydrates, which is usually followed by a lack of energy as the body digests these chemicals. Also, eating lots of fat can cause people to put on weight, which may lower their self-esteem.

There are many ways to manage diet for better physical and mental health. One way is to eat three regular meals a day with a healthy balance of fruit, vegetables, and whole grains. Another is to avoid snacks and excessive caffeine-rich foods such as coffee, chocolate, and tea. People should also drink four to eight cups of water a day. This helps with cell function and also helps avoid constipation. Some people find that certain food supplements lessen depression symptoms. Helpful supplements include folate, vitamin B12, fish oil, and the extract of a plant called St. John's wort.

Exercise and Sleep

Everyone has their preferred form of exercise, from hiking or swimming to skateboarding or gardening. The important thing is that it is fun, so you want to do it, and that it is also effective. Effective exercise will get you slightly out of breath, but not so much that you cannot talk while doing it. Of course, this depends on a person's age, general fitness, weight, and many other factors. Regular exercise keeps us fit and makes our bodies release endorphins.

Endorphins are the feel-good chemicals that boost mood. Exercise also tires us out so that we sleep better. Some people with depression wear step-counting fitness devices such as Fitbits. These devices may motivate them to exercise, even when they lack the energy and interest.

Water and exercise are two cornerstones of healthy living.

GENE STORIES

"Taking up running felt dreadful, but six months in, I know every step I run has been a step closer to feeling better thanks to endorphins. It is a simple equation: I feel down, so I run. Afterward my depression lifts, sometimes for days."

—Xavier, age thirty-eight

Helping Yourself and Others

Living with depression can be a big challenge. People can cope with it by using strategies to help themselves, and also by reaching out to other people. These people can be friends, family members, and other people who also experience depression or other mental illnesses. Sharing experiences, emotions, and practical tips for moderating symptoms can be an enormous help.

Survival Strategies

People with depression can turn to many strategies that have been helpful for others with the condition.

Simplify your life: Cut back obligations, set reasonable and achievable goals, and give yourself permission to do less when you feel down.

Write it down: Keeping a mood and thoughts diary, on paper or online as a blog, may improve your mood by allowing you to express pain, anger, fear, or other emotions.

Manage the stress: When you feel stress building, try methods to calm down, such as meditation, yoga, tai chi, or listening to calming music.

Plan your days: Without a plan, a day can seem worryingly full of tasks for someone who lacks energy and feels emotionally low. Use sticky notes as reminders of the most important tasks you need to complete during the day.

Using an organizer can help people with depression to plan their days and goals, chart their moods, and take control of their lives.

Reach Out to Others

Living with depression can be an isolating experience, but reaching out to others can help greatly. Some people with depression are comfortable talking to family and close friends about how they feel. Other people may find it easier to join a support group. These are groups of people who also have the condition. They can be national or local in scope, and may be connected with hospitals, clinics, churches, colleges, or workplaces. Talking to people who face similar problems can help people realize they are not alone. Support groups also give people the chance to share ideas for coping and learn from others who know what they are going through.

Support groups can help depression sufferers to work through their issues.

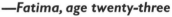

GENE STORIES

"A close friend really helped me when I was suffering with depression. She didn't think she was doing anything special, but what she did meant so much. She got in touch regularly just for a quick chat. I wasn't always in a place to answer, but I needed that so much. Whenever I said I was fine and coping, or pushed her away, she knew I wasn't and gave me a hug, or gave me the chance to talk. When I tried to cancel a get-together, she put the effort in to make it happen. She was always there for me."
—Fatima, age twenty-three

Chapter 6

Depression and Gene Therapy

In the future, people living with depression may be able to lessen the symptoms and escape the deep low moods of the illness by altering their genes. This may be possible because scientists have found ways to swap out mutations causing illnesses and replace them with healthy versions. This is known as gene therapy.

Gene Therapy

Gene therapy targets particular genes in a living thing. Scientists first identify a mutated section of DNA on a gene that is not functioning properly and might be causing a health problem. They then replace

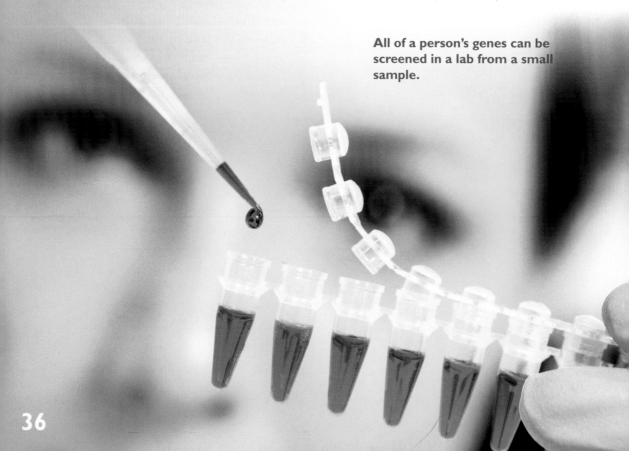

All of a person's genes can be screened in a lab from a small sample.

it with a new, functioning gene. The technique of editing or making changes to genes was first developed in the 1970s. However, it is only in recent times that more powerful computers and better laboratory techniques for gene editing have been available for scientists to use. Gene therapy is not yet used to treat depression, but it has already been successful in treating some illnesses. For example, gene therapy can shrivel and shrink some skin cancer tumors. As well, some people with Parkinson's disease experienced improved muscle control after having gene therapy to boost dopamine neurotransmitter production.

Knowing Genes

Scientists have so far identified more than twenty-one thousand genes in every human. Each gene is in a different location on one of the twenty-three chromosomes, and each has a different job to do for our bodies. For example, specific genes may cause cells to make particular proteins to build and repair themselves, or may affect the way sets of cells work together. This identification process is the result of the combined efforts of scientists worldwide looking at the patterns of around three billion chemical code units in human chromosomes. Many gene functions have been discovered, but much remains to be learned about how different genes interact.

GENE STORIES

"When I was ten years old my father took his own life. Later, my brother, my mother, and then I were all diagnosed with depression, too. It took a while to tease apart the grief we felt for my father's loss and our depression illness. It seemed like people thought we were weak for not dealing with the grief, and that the depression was our fault. So it's a comfort that scientists and the wider world are beginning to accept the genetics, because it legitimizes depression as a real illness."

—India, age twenty

How Gene Therapy Works

Gene therapy uses a person's own cells to treat illness, but it needs the help of viruses. If you have ever had a cold sore, then you have been attacked by a virus. Viruses are incredibly small living things, much smaller than bacteria.

Courier Service

Scientists can use modified viruses as couriers, or delivery services, for sections of DNA. Viruses have a small amount of DNA in genes protected inside a protein layer. They can only reproduce once they get inside other living cells. They then use energy from the host cell to start making copies of their genetic material. To modify a virus, scientists first remove any of the virus's own genes that cause sicknesses in people, such as the piece of DNA that causes painful lip sores in the cold sore virus. They replace them with the normal functioning gene. The virus can then "infect" human cells with this normal gene. The normal version replaces the mutated gene.

Where It Happens

The first part of gene therapy happens in laboratories, when scientists introduce viruses into unique cells called stem cells. These are unspecialized cells that can divide over and over, but can also turn into specialized cells with distinct functions. Scientists can get stem cells

Scientists can plan exactly where on chromosomes to replace mutated genes using gene therapy techniques.

from different places around the body, such as bone marrow and skin. They put the stem cells into a solution containing the viruses and also chemicals that help the stem cells divide quicker. After washing off the solutions, scientists can then inject the cells containing the normal gene into the person receiving gene therapy. Once inside the body, the normal copy of the gene will be passed on to other cells.

Testing therapies on lab animals, such as mice, can help scientists develop safe procedures.

Gene Genies

Injection of gene-transporting viruses into brains has showed promise in treating Parkinson's disease. Now scientists have demonstrated that the technique can reverse depression symptoms in mice. Researchers first bred mice without a gene called p11. They found that these mice showed signs of depression. The researchers then injected viruses containing p11 into a part of the limbic system called the nucleus accumbens, also known as the pleasure center. This part releases dopamine. Dopamine levels control likes and dislikes. The injected mice showed an increased effort and greater interest in challenges, consistent with less depression.

Challenges and Controversies of Gene Therapy

Gene therapy for depression is promising, but it is a more challenging and controversial therapy than antidepressants, for example. The techniques can work well in an artificial laboratory setting but are more difficult to predict in patients in the real world.

Beating the Shield

The body's defensive shield, the immune system, is populated by a mobile army of white blood cells. When white blood cells detect an attack by other organisms such as viruses, they defend our body's cells. Some white blood cells search for and destroy the viruses. Others create proteins to recognize the attackers to speed up defenses in future attacks. The viruses used in gene therapy can be recognized as intruders, too, even though they are not introducing a harmful disease. When your immune system goes into attack mode, your body uses up lots of energy so you feel exhausted. An immune attack can also cause inflammation of tissue and even failure of organs such as the liver. This is why scientists work hard to find viruses that are less likely to trigger an immune response.

Sensitive Tissue

Many normal medicines can be injected into the blood. The blood circulates them around the body to where they are useful. But the parts of the limbic system responsible for depression are hidden deep inside the brain. There is a barrier between blood and brain that gene therapy transporters, such as viruses, cannot pass. Getting edited cells into this sensitive tissue involves injection with needles. This is potentially harmful because physical damage could affect the way a patient experiences moods, thoughts, memories, and other aspects of the brain's function.

Controversies

Gene therapy is controversial for several reasons. One is that it opens the possibility for misuse. Depression is an illness that is thought of as being bad, and it seems straightforward to want to cure it through gene therapy. However, who decides what is normal and abnormal in a person's set of genes? Could the use of gene therapy make society less tolerant of people who are different, and have different abilities? Also, currently, gene therapy is performed on normal body cells. But what if future gene therapy was performed on sperm and egg cells to prevent them from passing on illnesses such as depression? Is it fair to decide the fate of future generations, especially as scientists are not fully aware of how different genes interact?

There is a naturally wide variation in characteristics between individuals and between genders. Could gene therapy narrow this variety?

Success for Depression Sufferers

The ultimate success of gene therapy for people with depression would be their illness receding into the background of their lives, rather than dominating the foreground. However, scientists and doctors will need to carry out trials to test the safety and effectiveness of gene therapy for depression before it can be put into use.

The Long Road

Long-term studies on large numbers of people will give scientists a better idea of how gene therapy affects a person's health and brain function. There are various pitfalls to avoid on this long road to safe gene therapy. For example, gene therapy relies on accurately delivering genes to particular places on chromosomes. If an introduced gene replaces the wrong piece of DNA, it might turn a normal cell into a cancer cell. Another pitfall is that changing one aspect of the brain could change another aspect. If a therapy increases neurotransmitter supply to reduce depression, could this changed brain chemistry have unexpected effects on memory, logic, or brain development?

Personalized Gene Therapy

Some people with depression are helped by one type of antidepressant, but others suffer unpleasant side effects and gain little benefit from the same drug. Because of these individual differences, some doctors think that personalized gene therapy is the way to go. Neurons grown from a person's own stem cells could be tested in laboratories for tolerance to different antidepressants, so doctors know which drugs to prescribe. By turning genes off and on in neurons in the laboratory, scientists may be able to determine how genes work together to control what goes on in an individual's brain and keeps them healthy.

In the future, people with depression may no longer be dependent on antidepressants and psychological therapies to get them through their depressive episodes.

Gene Genies

In a 2015 study at **Northwestern Medicine** in Illinois, researchers used gene therapy to reduce depression symptoms in mice. They did this by changing the electrical activity of neurons in the brain. The scientists surgically injected a virus carrying a gene that turns off **HCN** channel function into the hippocampus. That part of the limbic system is important for learning, memory, and emotional regulation. **HCN** channels are like gates in neurons that control the flow of messages. When the **HCN** channels stopped working, the mice behaved as though they had been given antidepressant medications. Scientists hope that such therapy might be developed into a human gene therapy in the future. The therapy would be delivered through pills rather than potentially damaging brain injections. That will be especially useful for people who have depression but do not respond to antidepressants.

Hope for the Future

Today, depression is widely acknowledged and treated as a real illness. It is not considered a weakness that people can choose to dismiss. With good treatment, effective and varied coping strategies, and compassionate support, anyone who has depression can feel better.

Living with Depression

Depression is not a permanent state of being. Even if the illness is always there, it comes as depressive episodes that have periods of

With successful treatment, individuals with depression can experience normal life with its range of ups and downs—but hopefully more ups than downs!

GENE STORIES

"I've been through the worst my mind can throw at me, yet I have realized something very important: depression is a liar. Therapies help me to see its lies. Then the heaviness gets lighter, and the world becomes brighter."
—*Terrence, age twenty-six*

Gene Genies

The stomach and intestines contain millions of bacteria that not only assist in digestion, but are also thought to be critical in establishing and maintaining the immune system. Scientists have recently discovered that gut bacteria make neurotransmitters which can send signals to the brain through a major nerve from the stomach called the vagus nerve. Researchers in Canada studied volunteers with irritable bowel syndrome—a condition in which people suffer with abdominal pain, diarrhea, constipation, and also often depression. They gave half these volunteers a probiotic supplement containing the bacteria *Bifidobacterium*, and the other half received an identical supplement without the bacteria. Depression symptoms improved in nearly two-thirds of the volunteers who were given the probiotic.

feeling better in between. Therefore, people can still live their lives and work to attain their goals. Having depression does not need to keep someone from going to college, taking that dream trip, having a satisfying and rewarding career, or having a family.

Changing Therapies

In the future, better antidepressants and new therapies will emerge to treat depression more effectively. Scientists are identifying more and more genes involved in clinical depression that might be treated with gene therapy. The Australian Genetics of Depression Study, which hopes to get around 200,000 participants, is likely to become is the world's largest genetic investigation. Already, they have analyzed genetic content of the chromosomes from the saliva samples of more than 10,000 Australians with depression. From that data, researchers hope to identify between 50 and 100 genes that influence a person's risk of developing clinical depression. The ultimate aim is to move on from therapies to treat symptoms. They aim to develop new, more effective, personalized treatments directly targeting the gene mutations that cause brain changes leading to depression.

Glossary

allergens Substances such as pollen that cause an allergic reaction from the immune system.

antidepressants Drugs that reduce symptoms of depression.

anxiety Deep worry, unease, and nervousness about something happening or about to happen.

bacteria Tiny living things that can cause disease.

bipolar disorder Mental illness in which people experience depressive and manic episodes.

bone marrow A soft substance that fills the spaces inside bones, which in adults also produces new blood cells.

cancer A disease caused by abnormalities in body cells.

chromosomes Parts of a cell that contain the genes which control how we grow and how we look.

cognitive behavioral therapy (CBT) Talk therapy used to treat depression and anxiety by changing the way a person thinks and behaves.

depressive episodes Periods of very low mood.

DNA Short for deoxyribonucleic acid, DNA contains the instructions an organism needs to develop, live, and reproduce.

epidemiologists Doctors specializing in patterns of disease.

genes Parts of cells that control or influence the way a person looks, grows, and develops.

heritability The degree to which a trait is capable of being inherited.

hormones Chemical substances produced in the body that control and regulate the activity of certain cells or organs.

immune system A system of body parts such as white blood cells that work to protect the body against disease.

inflammation Swelling and redness, caused by immune system activity.

inheriting Receiving from a parent or other relative.

insomnia Inability to sleep.

limbic system A system of nerves and networks in the brain concerned with instinct and mood.

mutations Significant changes in the structure of genes.

neglect Not being looked after properly by caregivers.

nervous system The network of nerve cells and fibers that transmits nerve impulses between parts of the body.

neurons Bundles of nerve fibers that carry messages between the brain and the rest of the body.

neurotransmitters Substances that transmit messages between neurons.

postpartum depression Depression suffered usually by mothers after childbirth.

post-traumatic stress disorder Mental health condition resulting from experiencing or seeing a terrifying event.

predetermined Decided in advance.

psychiatrist Doctor who diagnoses and treats mental illnesses.

psychological Relating to the mind, or the mental or emotional state.

psychotherapy Psychological rather than medical treatment of mental disorder, usually through communication with a therapist.

psychotic symptoms Mental confusion about reality such as hallucinations, delusions, or paranoia.

seasonal affective disorder (SAD) Type of depression linked to light levels in certain seasons.

self-esteem Confidence in one's own worth or abilities.

self-harm Injuring yourself on purpose.

serotonin Type of neurotransmitter involved in controlling mood and emotion in the limbic system.

side effect An additional and usually unwanted effect of drugs, chemicals, or other medical treatment.

suicidal Wanting to end your own life.

symptoms Changes in the body or mind caused by a disease or health condition.

trigger Cause to happen.

viruses Tiny organisms that invade and live in body cells and cause disease.

For Further Reading

Balinson, Andrea. *Depression, Anxiety, and Bipolar Disorders*. Broomall, PA: Mason Crest, 2018.

Brignall, Richard. *Champion for Health: How Clara Hughes Fought Depression to Win Olympic Gold*. Toronto, ON: James Lorimer & Company Ltd., 2016.

Crutchley, Lee. *How to Be Happy (Or at Least Less Sad): A Creative Workbook*. New York, NY: TarcherPerigee, 2015.

Parys, Sabrina. *Everything You Need to Know About Stress and Depression*. New York, NY: Rosen Young Adult, 2018.

Scarlet, Janina, and Wellinton Alves. *Superhero Therapy: Mindfulness Skills to Help Teens and Young Adults Deal with Anxiety, Depression, and Trauma*. Oakland, CA: New Harbinger Publications, 2017.

Sedley, Ben. *Stuff That Sucks: A Teen's Guide to Accepting What You Can't Change and Committing to What You Can*. Oakland, CA: Instant Help Books, 2017.

Toner, Jacqueline B., and Claire A.B. Freeland. *Depression: A Teen's Guide to Survive and Thrive*. Washington, DC: Magination Press, 2016.

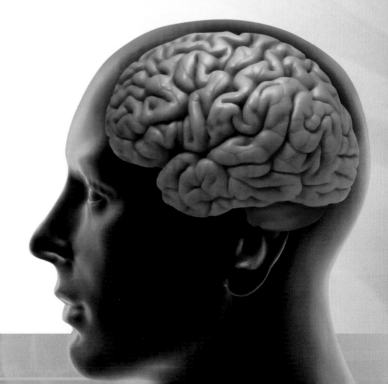

Index